IRELAND:
Beyond Leprechauns

Interdisciplinary Activities

Grades 2 through 8

by
Mary Ellen Sweeney, Ph.D.

ISBN: 978-0-9907759-2-8

View: www.amazon.com/books to order additional copies

IRELAND: Beyond Leprechauns
Interdisciplinary Activities, Grades 2 through 8

CONTENTS

Introduction

Many teachers and parents carry forward the yearly American tradition of building leprechaun traps and sprinkling fairy dust prior to classroom St. Patrick's Day celebrations. One year, two seventh graders in my charge in Omaha, Nebraska raised their hands a day or two after St. Patrick's Day, attesting to the sighting of leprechauns after a build-up by me with fables and activities about Ireland. Their raised hands were a testimony to my leprechaun indoctrination. An appreciation of all things Irish, including leprechauns, started early for me as St. Patrick's Day was celebrated at Epiphany Grade School in Miami, Florida with a school holiday and carnival. The Epiphany parish priests were from Ireland, because Miami was considered mission territory. The I.H.M. Sisters, our teachers were from the North, the Philadelphia area and proud of their most-certain Irish heritage.

I was raised in a predominately Irish parish, school and family. My great grandmother, Mary Anne Costello Cavanaugh was an emigrant from Ireland from the townland of Killsallagh near Glennamaddy and Tuam. Her family emigrated to Iowa. I was fortunate to have met my Great-Grandmother Cavanaugh, several times.

After five personal trips to Ireland, gathering information and activities with school-aged children in mind, I dare to present this 22 lesson-collection for a deeper look at Ireland. Loving leprechauns, fairies, superstitions, and St. Patrick is only a beginning experience of the Irish culture. I am not an expert or scholar of Ireland, but I am a proud descendent. Activities presented here have been applied and field-tested in the classroom on eager students. The activities have been accepted with enthusiasm. Completing some or all the activities in this book will prepare students to:

- Locate Ireland on a world map for the rest of their lives,

- Know that human life may be traced to 7,000 B.C. in Ireland,

- Speak a few words in Gaelic,

- Appreciate UNESCO and other important sites in Ireland,

- Try to understand how a community of Monks thrived in beehive huts on Michael Skellig (island),

- Understand the chronology of group after group that conquered the defenseless Irish,

- Recognize the Celts and the High Kings in Ireland from 400-1200 AD,

- Explore the architecture and purposes of 30,000 Irish castles,

- Study how Patrick, a captured Welsh nobleman turned slave, valued learning and education and bridged the Celtic and Christian eras by knowing, living, and valuing the Celtic culture,

- Value the Irish Monks and scholars who saved and recorded western civilization from the destruction of Barbarians because of their love of literature, learning, calligraphy, and art,

- o Understand the Potato Famine and how a failed crop for three years could devastate a population,

- o Explain the differences between emigration and immigration,

- o Inquire into the building and demise of the unsinkable Titanic,

- o Delve into the efforts of the human spirit of a long list of Irish freedom seekers that lead to the 1916 War of Independence,

- o Write some limericks and appreciate the contributions of W.B. Yeats and other Irish-born writers,

- o Interpret Irish ballads and songs and learn a few steps of Irish dance that will literally take anyone's breath away, and

- o Take the final challenge and build an itinerary for an individual, a class or group or family trip to Ireland!

The lessons are presented in a format for easy implementation for classroom teachers and/or parents who are challenged and pressured beyond reason. The lessons may also be explored by students from all over the world traveling to Ireland. Home school educators may find this book useful. Primary and secondary references listed in the "Reference" section may be accessed through local libraries and on the internet. The activities are intended to enhance students' knowledge of Ireland beyond leprechaun experiences. Leveled activities will challenge all learners in grades 2 through 8. Students may elect to springboard, brainstorm, or differentiate their own approach to learning about the topics in the various lessons in this book. The content is both deep and lighthearted. Students will surely enjoy the process of learning about the Irish people: their hardships, challenges, merriment, mischief, and resiliency!

Consumers of these activities are encouraged to send their positive feedback and suggestions for improvement, corrections, and ideas for additional activities for future editions to: mesween4@gmail.com.

Lesson 1: Ireland: What Do You Know?

Some students may actually know where Ireland is located on a world map. But many do not know. Other students may have traveled to Europe or Ireland, and some students may have Irish ancestors, friends, or neighbors.

Students will complete a KWLQ with prior knowledge about:

- o What they **know** about Ireland,
- o **What** they would like to learn about Ireland,
- o What they did **learn** after studying Ireland with the activities in this book.

Students will complete the KWLQ as one of the final activities in this book. They may have further **questions** about Ireland, and they may indicate them, as well as throughout the course of this study of Ireland.

Objective: Students will complete a pre-assessment about what they already know about Ireland.

Materials:

- o **KWLQ** Form on the following page
- o Folder or file for student work for the study of Ireland

Steps:

1. Students will be given a copy of the **KWLQ Form** for a pre-assessment of what they already know about Ireland. A discussion before or after the completion of the KWLQ may help students make personal connections with the course of study about Ireland.

2. Students will review completed KWLQ Forms together.

3. Students will be mindful about what they would like to learn about Ireland through this course of study. Students may use the KWLQ to track their interests and to remind the teacher of those topics of curiosity.

4. Students will keep the KWLQ in a personal folder that they will use for this unit of study. They will return to the KWLQ form throughout the activities and, then they will use it as a post-assessment in Lesson 21.

Evaluation: A student's completed **KWLQ** form or pre-assessment will indicate prior learning about Ireland.

Student Name _____

KWLQ: IRELAND

K What do you **KNOW**?	W **WHAT** do you want to learn?	L What did you **LEARN**?	Q **QUESTIONS** you still have?

Lesson 2: Irish Vocabulary: Gaelic and English

Students may have fun learning Irish vocabulary words in Gaelic. Students with an aptitude to learn new languages will especially enjoy this activity.

Objective: Students will record vocabulary words that are pertinent to a study of Ireland, and they will be able to speak several Gaelic words.

Materials:

- **ABC Vocabulary Chart** on the following page. Additional sheets may be added.
- *The Short Course: Speak Irish to Learn Irish.* (1999). Recorded Books, LLC.
- *Spoken World Irish: A Complete Course for Beginners.* (2009). New York, New York: Living Language, Random House.

Steps:

Students will:

1. Collect vocabulary words in Gaelic and English as the study of Ireland progresses.
2. Periodically share gathered vocabulary words.
3. At various intervals, gather the vocabulary charts and have a spelling bee!
4. Keep **ABC Vocabulary Charts** in their folders.
5. Have fun with "Irish" or "Gaelic" language courses. CDs may be checked out from public libraries.

Evaluation: Students will be able to pronounce several words in Gaelic. They will complete the vocabulary chart with meaningful words like the Gaelic greetings for welcome and good health. They may compete in periodic spelling bees.

Challenge: Students may create a Wordle (http://www.wordle.net/create) with the vocabulary word collection. Students may check out (www.puzzlemaking.com) to explore a word search or other puzzle once the vocabulary words are collected.

Student Name _____   Topic: IRELAND

ABC Vocabulary Chart

A		N	
B		O	
C		P	
D		Q	
E		R	
F		S	
G		T	
H		U	
I		V	
J		W	
K		X	
L		Y	
M		Z	

Lesson 3: Where in the World is Ireland?

Many students are not able to locate Ireland on a world map. This activity will allow them to locate Ireland on a world map for the rest of their lives!

Objective: Students will be able to locate Ireland on a world map. They will compare and contrast Ireland's geographical location with other countries. They will make generalizations about Ireland's location.

Materials:

Map book for classroom use like:

- *Ready-to-Go Super Book of Outline Maps.* (2000). New York, NY.: Scholastic, Inc.
- *Maps! The World and United States.* (1999). Riverside, CA: Teacher's Friend Publications, Inc.
- Or a World Atlas
- Or check out the websites below for maps for classroom use.
  - **World Map:** http://bit.do/bLLqc
  - **Map of Europe:** http://bit.do/bLLqo
  - **Map of Ireland:** http://bit.do/bLLqv
  - **Venn Diagram: Free Venn Diagram:** http://bit.do/bLLqB

Steps:

1. The following maps will be provided for each student by the teacher:
   - World Map
   - Map of Europe
   - Map of Ireland

2. Students will begin with the **World Map.** They will identify and label Ireland's location and then they will outline the seven continents. Students will identify the continent where Ireland is located.

3. Next, students will locate **Ireland** on the **Map of Europe**. With a partner, students may make at least 5 observations about Ireland's location, and then they may verbally share their observations.

4. With a partner, on the **Venn Diagram** (copied for each group) students will make five comparisons and state five contrasts that Ireland has with another country of the group's choice. Students will share comparisons and contrasts with the larger group.

5. Finally, students will draw the boundaries of the Republic of Ireland in green, and then Northern Ireland in orange. Students will label the capital cities of the Republic and Northern Ireland. Students will label the major rivers, surrounding seas, mountain ranges, The Burren, Giant's Causeway, Connemara, Dingle, Ring of Kerry, Skellig Islands, and major cities on their map of Ireland.

Evaluation: Student/s will complete three maps and a Venn Diagram and make assumptions about the geographical location of Ireland. Students will be able to locate Ireland on a world map for the rest of their lives!

Challenge: Students may research the history behind the flag of Ireland. First, they may draw a picture of the Irish flag, and then they may retell what the colors stand for on the Irish flag.

Lesson 4: History of Irish UNESCO Sites

Objective: Students will be able to identify and create a chart displaying the 2 UNESCO sites in Ireland.

Materials:

- o Definition of UNESCO
- o Computer access to information about UNESCO sites

Steps:

Students will:

1. Research the definition of UNESCO.

2. Identify the 2 official UNESCO sites plus the nominated sites in Ireland.

3. Construct a chart and categorize at least 5 characteristics of the 2 UNESCO sites in Ireland. Compare and contrast the 2 official sites.

4. Include drawings on their chart or add postcards if they have the good fortune to be in Ireland and visit the UNESCO sites.

Evaluation: Students will be able to share their chart of at least 2 UNESCO sites in Ireland. Students will be able to discuss the characteristics of each unique site.

Note to Teacher:

Nominated UNESCO World Heritage sites in Ireland include:

- The Burren (2010)
- The Historic City of Dublin (2010)
- The Céide Fields and North West Mayo Boglands (2010)
- Western Stone Forts (2010)
- The Monastic City of Clonmacnoise and its Cultural Landscape (2010)
- Early Medieval Monastic Sites (2010)
- The Royal Sites of Ireland: Cashel, Dún Ailinne, Hill of Uisneach, Rathcroghan Complex, and Tara Complex (2010)

Challenge: Students will add two of the additional nominated World Heritage sites to the constructed chart.

Lesson 5: Irish Geographical and Historical Phenomenon

Some students are born with an interest in rocks. This lesson will particularly appeal to them!

Objective: Students will be able to identify other important historical and geographical phenomenon in Ireland.

Materials:

- o Computer access
- o Encyclopedias
- o Resource books including:
  - Lavelle, Des. (1999) *The Skellig Story: Ancient Monastic Outpost*. Dublin, Ireland: The O'Brien Press.
  - Moreton, Cole (2000). *Hungry for Home: Leaving the Blaskets: A Journey from the Edge of Ireland*. New York: Penguin Putnam, Inc.
  - Craven, Rachael (2009). *Spirit of the Causeway Coast*. Somerset, Great Britain.
  - Student-made Graphic organizer (Topic Bubble in the middle of a page with 5 or 6 outlying Supporting Detail Bubbles)

Steps:

Students will:

1. Research at least 5 of the following historical and geographical sites in Ireland, in groups of two or three students:
   - Giant's Causeway,
   - Cliffs of Mohr,
   - Burren,
   - Ringforts,
   - Aran Islands,
   - Dingle Penisula,
   - Dun Aengus

- Michael Skellig, Glens of Antrim,
- Ring of Kerry,
- Great Blasket Island,
- Other: _____

2. Draw a Graphic Organizer for note taking. Students may create a "Topic Bubble" in the middle of a piece of paper with 5 or 6 outlying bubbles to record their discovered details.

3. Share their Graphic Organizers with the entire class once they are completed. The teacher may display the completed graphic organizers on butcher-block paper on a wall in the classroom.

4. Collect their graphic organizers and either display them or store them in their folder.

Evaluation: Each student will be able to recall a minimum of five details of the historical and geographical phenomenon of the Irish sites listed above.

Lesson 6: Colonization of Ireland

Students may have fun with this activity: charting the first explorers, and then identifying the first inhabitants of Ireland!

Objective: Students will develop and experience a timeline of the different groups who explored and settled in Ireland from 7,000 B.C. to the present.

Materials:

- o Computer access for research
- o Books like:
  - Broderick, Mary (1989). *History of Cobh (Queenstown) Ireland.* Cork City, Ireland: Carraig Print.
  - Scanlan, Margaret (2006). *Culture and Customs of Ireland.* Westport, CT: Greenwood Press.
  - A simple, class-created, wall-size Timeline like:

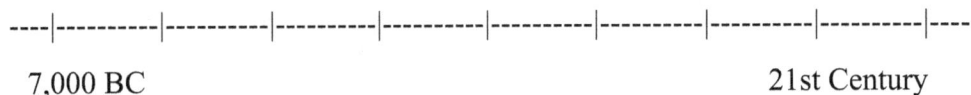

----|----------|----------|----------|----------|----------|----------|----------|----------|-----

7,000 BC   21st Century

Steps:

Students will:

1. Create a timeline from 7,000 B.C. using resource books like Broderick (1989: 2-36) or Scanlan (2006) and read about the six colonization periods. Broderick writes about the island where the harbor of Cobh (or Queenstown) is located. The information will guide learners to an easier understanding of the groups that came to Ireland. She explains why and when they came. Scanlan provides a timeline with major events from 7,000 B.C. to the 21st century.

2. Produce a classroom timeline, and they will each make a list of ten "I Didn't Know" statements.

Evaluation: From a class-created timeline, students will be able to retell facts that they learned about the exploration of Ireland since 7,000 B.C.

Lesson 7: Islands: Pick an Island

Although Ireland is an island onto itself, a trip to Ireland is more complete with a boat ride to one of the many outlying islands. A trip to at least one of the islands will be added to an Ireland trip itinerary in the final activity (Lesson 22) in this book.

Objective: Students will enjoy themselves experiencing the seven islands listed through Google Earth. They will add at least seven facts to their notebooks.

Materials:

- o   Google Earth access
- o   Encyclopedias including Wikipedia
- o   YouTube

Steps:

Student will:

1.   Pick an island! In small groups, students will research the following islands using the resources listed in the materials section and Google Earth.

- Skelling Michael Island
  - Find the monastery rock formations at this UNESCO site. Discover the Michael Skellig and Lighthouse museum on this island.
- Blasket Islands
  - Explore the rock formations until you find the Reclining Man.
- Raithlin Island
  - Travel the ferry trip on the water from Ballycastle to Raitlin.
- Aran Islands
  - Encounter Dun Aengus, the prehistoric ring fort from 1,100 B.C.
- Tory Island
  - Surf to locate the "Evil Eye, "Wishing Stone," or the pre-Christian Cross.
- Achill Island
  - Locate Clew Bay where the O'Malley tribe held off the Vikings.

Ponder this Question:

Why would archeologists and anthropologists be interested in Gaelic monasteries, and the artifacts and monuments on Skellig Michael, Aran Islands, Tory Island, and Achill Island?

Lesson 8: Irish High Kings and Brian Boru

DNA results are revealing Irish King lineage for many Irish descendants. Brian Boru became the last High King in 1002. His patriotism brought warring clans together for the only time in Irish history. The following lesson will expose students to the High Kings of Ireland, including Brian Boru.

Objective: Students will learn about Brian Boru and/or other High Kings of Ireland.

Materials:

Research materials including:

- o Time-Life Books (Editors) (1998). *What Life Was Like Among Druids and High Kings (Celtic Ireland AD 400-1200)*. New York, New York: Time-Life Inc.

- o http://www.yourirish.com/history/ancient/high-kings-of-ireland

- o https://en.wikipedia.org/wiki/Brian_Boru

Steps:

Students will:

1. Try to locate a copy of the Time-Life book listed above and then read to understand and experience what daily life would have been like during the Druid and High Kings' era.

2. Define Druid and add it to the Ireland ABC Vocabulary list.

3. Use the websites above and read about the High Kings, especially the famous Brian Boru.

4. Read to discover what group Brian Boru aligned himself with to secure his territory.

5. Dramatize individually, in small groups or as a whole group what daily life would have been like during the reign of Brian Boru or other Irish High Kings.

Lesson 9: Irish Castles: History and Architecture

A visit or study of Ireland would not be complete without a close look at one or two of the 30,000 castles. Fortunately, they have been preserved and they are everywhere in Ireland! Students may explore one castle in-depth, gathering as much information as time and resources allow.

Objective: Students will learn about why and when castles were built in Ireland.

Materials:

- ○ Browsing Planner for Irish Castles following this lesson
- ○ Books like: Hart, Avery and Mantell, Paul (1998). *Knights and Castles: 50 Hands-On Activities to Explore the Middle Ages*. Nashville, TN: Williamson Publishing.
- ○ Computer access for exploring, browsing and fact gathering.
- ○ On-line resources: Try to find access to the 2016 Series "Tales of Irish Castles" viewed on PBS.

Steps:

1. Students will use the following questions to gather their research about castles in general:
   - What time period or era were castles first built in Ireland?
   - What materials were used to build castles?
   - What was the purpose of castles?
2. Students may complete the first step as a class or group. Then, students will choose a castle and answer the questions above, plus the additional questions listed below:
   - Trace the castle's ownership.
   - Discuss the location and the purpose of the castle.
   - Identify and retell legends or fables about the castle.
   - Find a list of possible castle choices at:
     https://en.wikipedia.org/wiki/List_of_castles_in_the_Republic_of_Ireland

Or students may select a castle from the short list below:

Possible Castle Choices:

- Malahide Castle (www.malahidecastleandgardens.ie)

- Castle Leslie Estate

- Blarney Castle (http://www.blarneycastle.ie)

- Lough Eske Castle

- Kylemore Abbey

- Ballynahinch Castle

- Ross Castle (http://www.heritageireland.ie/en/South-West/RossCastle)

- Hunt Museum

- Doe Castle (Clan Sweeney) (http://www.sweeneyclanchief.com/id8.htm)

Evaluation: Students will record their research efforts on the Browsing Planner for Irish Castles.

Challenge: Students may build a full or partial model of a castle and share the completed model with the class. Students may research about life in the castle and the function of the different rooms and share that information in a presentation to the class or group.

Use the book, *Knights and Castles: 50 Hands-On Activities to Explore the Middle Ages,* cited above for ideas.

Browsing Planner:

Irish Castles

Source of Information	Title	Author	Source Location
Primary Sources			
Secondary Sources			
Other Sources			

Lesson 10: Irish Celtic and Christian Periods

Patrick skillfully used his knowledge of the traditions and rituals of pagan Ireland to convert the Irish to Christianity. His years in captivity as an Irish slave allowed him to learn the language and to experience the culture of the people firsthand. That knowledge helped him to mesh the Gaelic ways with Christian beliefs and convert many of the Irish people to Christianity without negating the Celtic traditions.

Objective: Students will learn about the Irish Gaelic and Christian periods.

Materials:

o Broderick, Mary (1989). *History of Cobh (Queenstown) Ireland.* Cork City, Ireland: Carraig Print.

o Computers for on-line research

o DVD, "Patrick" (2007) narrated by Liam Neeson and Gabriel Byrne, commentator by Frank McCourt, directed by Pamela Mason Wagner.

Steps:

Students will:

1. Research for understanding about the Celtic and Christian periods in Ireland. They may refer to the Timeline developed in Lesson 6.

2. Create another Timeline for the Celtic and Christian periods.

3. View the DVD of "Patrick" (2009). This dramatic resource for the study of St Patrick is an interesting depiction and summary of the ways that Patrick learned Gaelic as a slave and used it to bridge the Celtic traditions with Christianity. Students will watch the entire DVD, checking for stereotypical myth busting. For example, students may find out if St. Patrick really did drive out snakes from Ireland? In small groups of students, have them develop 3 "true" and "false" statements. Then, collate the group work into one true and false quiz. Have students take the quiz informally as either individuals or as a class/group.

Evaluation: Students will exhibit their knowledge of the Celtic and Christian periods in Ireland by correctly answering a student-developed true and false quiz about St. Patrick.

Challenge: Students may make an iMovie of one of the scenes from the movie, "Patrick."

For middle school students: Students may start a book club and read: Cahill, Thomas (1995). *How the Irish Saved Civilization: The Untold Story of Ireland's Heroic Role from the Fall of Rome to the Rise of Medieval Europe.* New York, NY: Doubleday.

Lesson 11: The Book of Kells: An Irish Treasure

"The Book of Kells" was written in the late 600s A.D. by Celtic monks and it is a treasure of Ireland! The monks rescued and hid it during the Barbarian destruction of such learned works and writings throughout Europe. To be in the presence of "The Book of Kells" and to experience the display at Trinity College in Dublin is a wonder of the world. This masterpiece of Western calligraphy, with elaborate spirals and Celtic knot work, was at one time valued more for the artwork than for the content. The display at Trinity College is a modern exhibition and feat in itself.

Objective: Students will experience the artwork and content of "The Book of Kells."

Materials:

Books:

- o Simms, G.O. (ed.) (1986). *The Book of Kells*. England: Cheney & Sons Ltd.

- o Sibbett Jr., E. (1979). *Celtic Design Coloring Book*. Mineola, NY: Dover Publications, Inc., 1979.

Websites:

- o http://em.wikipedia.org/wiki/Book_of_Kells

- o http://www.dochara.com/places-to-visit/museums/trinity-college/

Steps:

Students will:

1. Read about the "Book of Kells" at: http://em.wikipedia.org/wiki/Book_of_Kells.

2. Observe, analyze, and possibly color some of the sample pictures that are contained in Sibbett's coloring book listed above.

3. Try to enlarge one of the pictures of the Book of Kells from Wikipedia or elsewhere for a student coloring experience and for an appreciation of the intricacies of the detailed design. Discuss where the monks might have obtained dye for colors. Contemplate how long a page may have taken to complete. Primarily the colors that were used include: white, red, yellow, green, blue, indigo, pink and purple. Discuss where and how the monks may have made dye for ink. Investigate where they obtained other materials (paper, pens) for "The Book of Kells."

Evaluation: Students will be able to describe "The Book of Kells."

Lesson 12: Calligraphy: Art and Penmanship Of The Irish Monks

Dennis Gallagher, an Irish Historian and Professor at Regis University in Denver, CO, a Colorado legislator, and Denver City Auditor stated that calligraphy runs through the veins of the Irish! Morgan Llywelyn (2010: 81) in *"Brendan: The Remarkable Life and Voyage of Brendan of Clonfert"* emphasizes the literary and artful contribution of the Irish Monks:

> "Until the coming of Christianity, knowledge had been passed down through the oral tradition for countless generations. The missionaries brought literacy to Ireland. As the monastic movement grew, monks were assigned to make copies of the Gospels. The Gaelic passion for exuberant patterns and vivid colors soon exited its influence; the manuscripts became works of art."

Students will be exposed to that art form in the following lesson.

Objective: Students will study calligraphy, explore the basic strokes, and try their hand on a piece or project or two. They may be able to write their name in the calligraphic style of their choice.

Materials:

- o Examples of "The Book of Kells" like Simms, G.O. (1986).
- o Beginning books on calligraphy: Winters, Eleanor. *1-2-3 Calligraphy! Letter and Projects for Beginners and Beyond.* (2006). New York: Sterling Children's Books.
- o YouTube demonstrations of basic calligraphy strokes.

Steps:

Students will:

1. Find examples of calligraphy, especially the Irish Monks' use of Gothic or Black Calligraphy from the Middle Ages. A book or internet example of "The Book of Kells" will be a helpful source for students to study the monks' flourish, decoration and detail.

2. Use beginning books of calligraphy and YouTube examples. Primary students may work on forming lower case lettering and intermediate or secondary students may learn to form lower- and upper-case lettering.

3. Over numerous days, explore the basic vocabulary of calligraphy including: pens, calligraphy paper, markers, posture, pen position, paper slanting and nibs.

4. Begin learning and practicing basic strokes together.

5. Work on a project together like making signs for their bedrooms or school table/desks.

6. Experiment with substitute handwriting exercises using italic handwriting as explained and demonstrated in Winter's book on p. 44.

7. Experience the importance of practice.

Evaluation: Students may be exposed to the basics of calligraphy. They will attempt the writing of their name on a sign of their choice, for example.

Challenge: After learning the basics of calligraphy with markers, students may try different nibs with indelible ink. Students will remember to tape the ink bottle to the work surface to avoid spillage.

This is an excellent time to find a personal resource who knows the ins and outs of calligraphy and ask them for a demonstration or assistance in person!

Lesson 13: Brendan: Courageous Saint, Scholar, and Explorer

Brendan was an Irish monk who just missed meeting Patrick. Patrick was one of the first non-native priests to spread Christianity in Ireland. Brendan, like Patrick is a famous native Irish saint. Brendan was a dedicated scholar, explorer, teacher, leader, and adventurer. He learned about people and places through his pilgrimages and voyages, rarely knowing where he was going. People flocked to hear his stories upon his return from any given solo pilgrimage or group voyage. He learned fishing and boat building by necessity.

Objective: Students will be able to recount and record an unlimited number of facts about Brendan's life including: his early life, life as one of the first Irish monks, and life as a fearless navigator and insatiable traveler.

Materials:

- Book: Llywelyn, Morgan (2010). *Brendan: The Remarkable Life and Voyage of Brendan of Clonfert.* New York: A Tom Doherty Associates Book.

Steps:

Students will:

1. Form a book club of advanced intermediate-aged and/or middle school (approximately grades 5-8) students. Students will be allocated approximately two weeks to read the book, and then one week for culminating activities to synthesize, analyze and connect with Brendan and his earthly activities.

2. Set the stage for the book by previewing it together. Students will notice the Druid legends and superstitions integrated throughout the book. Students will want to read through the following three activities (Jigsaw the Eight Elements of Culture, Senses Graphic Organizer and Products List) before reading the text.

3. Decide which activities to complete after reading the book:
   - The Cultural Jigsaw
   - The "Senses Graphic Organizer"
   - Activities of interest from the "Products List"

Jigsaw the Eight Elements of Culture

Each student will volunteer to complete one of the eight pieces of culture by recording the selected element of culture after reading about Brendan and his adventures. Share student observations with others.

Artifacts	**Stories, Myths, Superstitions**
Rituals, Rites, Ceremonies and Celebrations	**Heroes**
Symbols and Symbolic Action	**Beliefs and Assumptions**
Attitudes	**Rules, Norms, Ethical Codes and Values**

Senses Graphic Organizer

A student may use the "Senses Graphic Organizer" while reading the historic fictional account of Brendan's early life and later life experiences. Review the six senses and suggested questions to guide readings.

SEE What does the setting look like? What colors, textures, shapes do you see? What new vocabulary words would you use to describe what you see (currach, coracles, monastery, etc.)? _____ _____ _____	**SMELL** What do you smell? Describe the smells. How many smells are there? _____ _____ _____ _____
TOUCH What would the different objects in this area feel like? What words will help others to feel what you are feeling? _____ _____ _____ _____	**TASTE** What tastes might you experience as a character immersed in the setting of Brendan's life? Are there tasted here that you might like or dislike (hint: fish)? _____ _____ _____
HEAR What sounds do you hear? Describe the pitch of the sounds (high and/or low). _____ _____ _____	**FEEL** List some of Brendan's emotions. What are the emotions of others in this book setting? How would you have felt living in a monastery in Brendan's time? _____ _____ _____

Products List

Use the following list of products to further synthesize your thoughts after reading about Brendan. Students will:

Place yourself in Brendan's shoes and write a **diary entry.**	Tape an **interview** of Brendan for a radio show. If you can't find a partner, then be both Brendan and the interviewer.	Build a **collage** from magazine pictures or your own drawings of the visual images of the setting of this book.
Draw or create a monk's **costume** from this period.	Make a **rubbing** of an image from Brendan's culture to share with younger children.	Create a **timeline** from Brendan's birth to his death.
Create and perform a **skit** from one of the scenes from the book about Brendan.	On a **map**, trace Brendan's travels. Will the map include only Ireland?	Write and perform a **Monologue** from Brendan or any of the other characters in this book.
Research for a possible **song** of the monks or write your own song.	Research "**Ogham.**" Copy and share one of the designs.	**Student suggestion**: Share an idea of your own to summarize this book about Brendan.
Illustrate and retell about the Festival of Beltraine.	**Dramatize** how the Druids might have acted.	Identify a **monastery** that you might want to visit in Ireland. Add it to your itinerary in Lesson 22.
Use a **Venn Diagramm** to compare and contrast the roles of women and men in Brendan's life.	**Draw** the Giant Serpent described in Chapter 22 and retell that fable.	**Construct a model** of a coracle, curragh or clachan.
Name the 27 chapters since they are unnamed.	**Investigate** what "iolite" is and explain why it was packed by the monks.	**Draw** Preachan and tell stories about him.

Lesson 14: History: The Irish Potato Famine

Many of Irish descent who are traveling to Ireland will not find living relatives. Six million Irish emigrated to continents beyond Ireland between 1848 and 1950. Read and research how the black potatoes for three years caused death, destruction, and the departure of millions of Irish.

Objective: Students will be able to identify some of the causes of the Irish Potato Famine.

Materials:

- o Computer access
- o Resource books including encyclopedias:
    - Pastore, Clare (2001). *Journey to America: Fiona McGilray's Story: A Voyage from Ireland in 1849*. New York, New York: Berkley Jam Books.
    - Wilson, Laura (2000). *How I Survived the Irish Famine: The Journal of Mary O'Flynn*. Dublin, Ireland: Gill & Macmillan Ltd.
- o Giant classroom chart to post: Five Ws (who what, where, when, why) and One H (how) Form (see the following page)

Steps:

Students will:

1. Divide into 6 groups and will choose one of the Ws or H (who, what, where, when, why, how) and then conduct research for their part of "Irish Potato Famine."

2. Decide how they will record their part of the research.

3. Share with the rest of the class their findings and then post them on a giant classroom chart.

4. Read Laura Wilson's (2000) book listed above, as an option. They will pay attention to the **Glossary** on page 36. Students will want to add new words to their ABC Vocabulary Chart from Lesson 2.

Evaluation: Each student will be able to discuss their part of the study of "The Irish Potato Famine."

Challenge:

1. Students may research the origins of the potato and explain how the potato made its way to Ireland and became such an important Irish staple.

2. Students may discuss how the Irish Potato Famine caused widespread change in Ireland.

Five Ws and One H

Use this format to build a giant classroom wall display to complete a student group study of "The Irish Potato Famine".

WHO is the story about?	**TOPIC**	**WHAT** happened in the story?
WHEN did it take place?	_____ _____ _____ _____	**WHERE** did it take place?
WHY is this story important?		**HOW** did it happen?

Lesson 15: History: Irish Emigration to North America

Between 1848 and 1950 over six million Irish left Ireland. Fifty percent of the passengers departed from Cobh or Queenstown, the last port of the Titanic. This lesson will help students understand why the Irish left.

Objective: Students will understand the reasons why large numbers of Irish left their homeland.

Materials:

- o Encyclopedias, resource materials and books about the 19th century migration out of Ireland like:
  - Loughrey, Eithne. (1999) *Annie Moore: First in Line in America.* Dublin, Ireland: Mercier Press.
  - Miller, Kirby and Patricia Mulholland Miller. (2001) *Journey of Hope: The Story of Irish Immigration to America.* San Francisco, CA: Chronicle Books LLC.
  - Nolan, Janet. (2002). *The St. Patrick's Day Shillelagh.* Morton Grove, IL: Albert Whitman & Company. For grades 2 and 3.
  - Schneider, Mical (2001). *Annie Quinn in America.* Minneapolis, MN: Carolrhoda Books, Inc.
  - Moreton, Cole. (2000). *Hungry for Home: Leaving the Blaskets: A Journey from the Edge of Ireland.* New York, New York: Penguin Putnam, Inc.
- o Computer access for research including the following site:
  - Cobh/Queenstown – Heritage Museum
    - http://www.dochara.com/places-to-visit/museums/cobh-heritage-centre/
    - http://www.cobhheritage.com/

Steps:

Between 1848 and 1950 over 6 million Irish left Ireland, and 50 percent departed from Cobh or Queenstown.

1. Define immigration and emigration. Compare and contrast the definitions as it applies to Ireland in the mid-1800s. Check out the following website and then have a group discussion about it.
   - http://www.educationbug.org/a/immigration-vs-emigration.html

2. For primary students, read *The St. Patrick's Day Shillelagh* (2002) together.

3. Create a timeline. Summarize the shillelagh's owners' stories and appropriately place them on the timeline.

4. Research to discover why Annie Moore was given a $10 gold piece by New York City dignitaries upon her arrival at Ellis Island. Try: Loughrey, Eithne (1999). *Annie Moore: First in Line in America.* Dublin, Ireland: Mercier Press.

5. Statues honoring Annie Moore are located in Cobh and on Ellis Island. Check out the following website to experience the Irish heritage museum and to view Annie Moore's statue:

   - Cobh/Queenstown – Heritage Museum

   - http://www.dochara.com/places-to-visit/museums/cobh-heritage-centre/

6. Write a summary report about the reasons why so many people left Ireland in the 1840s. Explain how they were able to afford the trip to North America or Australia.

Evaluation: Students will write a summary report about the migration out of Ireland in the 19th century. They will include the causes of the emigration and an explanation of the difference between emigration and immigration.

Challenge:

Students may:

1. Dramatize a scene of Irish immigrants from one of the ships making the voyage to North America.

2. Imagine how Ireland would be today if the potato famine would not have happened and the Irish emigrants would have stayed in Ireland.

3. Form a Book Club (Grades 5 through 8) and read Morton, Cole (2000). *Hungry for Home: Leaving the Blaskets: A Journey from the Edge of Ireland.* New York, New York: Penguin Group. This non-fiction account of Blasket life has strong, descriptive imagery. Students will have a better understanding of the Blasket daily life and culture by reading this well-written literature. The following quote may inspire students to read this book:

   "Beside them in the light of a lamp, as the winter lays down its dark skirts for the evening, are some of the last remaining young men of the island, all but silent at the loss of a friend." (Morton, 2000: 24).

Lesson 16: The Titanic

Books about the Titanic are well read and worn because of student interest. Students will want to access the Titanic exhibit in Belfast via the web. They may add a visit to the Belfast exhibit of the Titanic on their itinerary in Lesson 22. A stop on the itinerary in Cobh for Michael Martin's "Titanic Trail" is strongly recommended as well. Cobh was the last port of the Titanic, before leaving for North America.

Objective: Students will learn basic facts about a high interest topic: **The Titanic**.

Materials:

- o Books for a Titanic Study:
    - Michael Martin (2001). *Titanic Trail*. Cork, Ireland: Collins Print and Packaging Ltd.
    - McKeown, Arthur (1996). *Titanic*. Dublin, Ireland: Poolbeg Press, Ltd.
    - Cartwright, R. (2011). *The Pitkin Guide to Titanic*. Andover, Hampshire: Pitkin Publishing.
- o Titanic Websites:
    - http://ultimatetitanic.com/
    - http://nmni.com/titanic/
    - http://titanicbelfast.com

Steps:

Students will want to spend days on this topic. After making resources available for learning about the Titanic, some activities for students may include:

1. Gathering information about the building, loading, and sailing of the Titanic to create a timeline. Students may present a Power Point or Prezi of facts and findings.

2. Composing and writing a song about the Titanic from an Irish passengers' point of view. Students may visit the following website to listen to passengers' accounts:
    - http://nmni.com/titanic

3. Writing and performing a play about the Titanic from one of the shipbuilder's point of view.

4. Constructing a model of the Titanic from clay or other student-selected materials.

5. Writing a business letter to the White Star Line to advise them on passenger safety.

6. Forming a book study for students in grades 5-8 and reading a novel about Maggie's experience on the Titanic. She was one of fourteen people from Addergoole who left on the Titanic. Students may trace and relive her experience in this historical fiction account: Gaynor, Hazel (2014). *The Girl Who Came Home*. New York: Harper Collins.

7. Proposing a method of demonstrating student knowledge about the Titanic to the teacher.

Evaluation: Students will demonstrate their learning about the Titanic through an activity of their choice.

Lesson 17: History: 1916 Irish Independence

This activity will easily take a week or more of Social Studies and Language Arts periods. This lesson will require time for in-depth study. Because of the emotional level of this information, the research may be reserved for mature intermediate and middle school students. Teachers are cautioned to provide a letter to parent/s and guardians prior to this lesson's study, due to the sensitive content that students may uncover during research. Parents guiding this lesson are advised to peruse the delicate nature of the historical information. Be forewarned that this material is of high interest for middle school students. Teachers and parents will want to have ongoing conversations about possible materials uncovered in the study of the 1916 Irish Independence.

Objective: Students will familiarize themselves with one of the historic figures or events of the struggle for independence from England, in the Easter Rising in 1916.

Materials:

- o Books, encyclopedias
- o Computer access
- o **Browsing Planner**, 1 per student or group
- o Clay Animation or Claymation information or purchased kits
- o Guest Speakers

Steps:

Students will:

1. Organize for research and use the Browsing Planner on the following page. After browsing, students will decide on a figure or event to study.

2. Network and possibly plan for **guest speakers** who are knowledgeable about the events that led to the Easter Rising in 1916. Universities with Irish scholars and representatives from Irish organizations may be a natural starting point to seek appropriate Irish guest speakers.

3. Examine the picture of the leaders of the Irish Republic of 1916 on the following page. Students will browse through Irish history and the suggested names and events. They may uncover other figures and events that may be negotiated with the teacher. Some of the figures and events include:

   - Patrick Pearse,
   - James Connolly,

- Michael Collins,

- Terence MacSwiney,

- J.J. O'Connell,

- Kevin Barry,

- The Forgotten Ten,

- Eamon deValera,

- Government of Ireland Act, 1920,

- Irish Home Rule Movement,

- Irish War of Independence

4. Create a **Claymation** (http://www.ikitmovie.com/49/about-us.htm) of one of the historic Irish figures and events that led to the **1916 Easter Rising**. A simple puppet show may be an alternative.

Challenge:

Students may:

1. Research and discuss how the Irish Volunteers became the Irish Republican Army, including their engaged warfare techniques. On the itinerary in Lesson 22, students may add a visit to the General Post Office in Dublin to experience the exhibit there about this event.

2. Investigate to find out why the Anglo-Irish Treaty of 1921 was not embraced by all Irish citizens. Students may research to find out "Why" and share their findings with the entire class.

3. Read the book: Llywelyn, Morgan (1998). *1916: A Novel of the Irish Rebellion*. New York: Tom Doherty Associates. Students may share with the class the two sides in this conflict.

4. Study another liberator's efforts, laying the groundwork for the people and events listed above is **Daniel O'Connell** (1775-1847). Read about his efforts for Catholic emancipation and for an Ireland free of British rule. O'Connell was known as "The Liberator" or "The Emancipator." Read about his efforts and causes and report back to the larger group in a format of student choice.

5. Recognize the Women who were the mothers and sisters of the heroes of the 1916 War of Independence. Research how Irish women contributed to other war efforts directly throughout Irish history. Begin at the following website: http://bit.do/Irishheroines. A contemporary female leader and former President of Ireland, **Mary McAleese** would make an interesting study for a student because of her Northern Ireland roots and her Catholic background.

6. View films. Middle school and high school students may want to watch part or all the following films:

   - "Jimmy's Hall" (PG-13, 2014)
   - "The Wind That Shakes the Barley" (PG-13, 2006)

Both films were directed by Ken Loach. Watch for the political, social, and economic tones in Ireland during the 1920s. Students may discuss their perceptions and reactions. Teachers will want to preview these films, due to content, prior to showing them to students. "Jimmy's Hall" is less violent than "The Wind That Shakes the Barley." Both movies are rated PG-13. Students may want to use the **Jigsaw of the Eight Elements of Culture** from Lesson 13 to view and discuss the contents of either or both films.

Tea towel used with permission from Allied Imports, www.alliedimports.com

Browsing Planner:

Irish Independence Figures and Events

Source of Information	Title	Author	Source Location
Primary Sources			
Secondary Sources			
Other Sources			

Lesson 18: Irish Literature and Storytelling

In previous lessons, students found that the Irish monks hid and copied invaluable manuscripts and documents of Western Civilization during the fall of the Roman Empire and the nonviolent take over by the Barbarians. Rightfully, Ireland is called the "Island of Saints and Scholars." In this lesson, students will delve into the past accomplishments of some of Ireland's famous writers. For storytelling and poetry, students will experience W.B. Yeats as well as Irish-born and raised Yeats' admirer, C.S. Lewis They both valued creativity and imagination.

W. B. Yeats (1865-1939) is buried in Sligo, and he is one Ireland's most famous poets. Students may research and share some of his writing, like "Belief and Unbelief." This poem is appropriate for all ages. In light of the motivation and name of this collection of activities, "Beyond Leprechauns," the aforementioned poem lends itself to a lively poetry read and discussion. Students may memorize several lines of an age-appropriate Yeats' poem. Students may recite it to any listening audience! Remember it for life.

This is the perfect time to invite a guest speaker or expert to talk about Ireland!

Objective: Students will learn about two of Ireland's famous writers: William Butler Yeats (1865-1939) and C.S. Lewis (1898-1963).

Materials:

- **Making Connections Chart**, following this lesson
- W.B. Yeats (2010 edition). *The Celtic Twilight: Faeries and Folklore.* Las Vegas, NV: IAP.
- C.S. Lewis. (2010 edition) *Chronicles of Narnia: The Magician's Nephew.* New York, NY: Harper Festival.
- Internet access for research:
- https://www.cslewis.com/us/ (includes C.S. Lewis organizations throughout Europe and the United States)
- https://www.poets.org/poetsorg/poet/w-b-yeats
- *Secret of Roan Innish.* DVD (1994)

Steps:

Students will:

1. Decide how they may group themselves to research the two famous authors. Many students may be familiar with C.S. Lewis' children's books. They may not be aware that he was born and raised in Northern Ireland.

2. Select a favorite fairy story from Yeats for a read aloud with younger students, like "Belief and Unbelief."

3. Read and research about the two writers using the materials listed above, or other discovered resources.

4. Memorize and recite several lines of an age-appropriate Yeats or C.S. Lewis poem or quote.

5. Have some fun writing limericks by first investigating their format at: www.gigglepoetry.com/poetryclass/limerickcontesthelp.html

6. Try to write a limerick with a partner. They may write a limerick about their partner's attributes or name.

7. Watch part of the DVD, "Secret of Roan Innish" (1994) with all ages. They will have a discussion about whether it is fiction or nonfiction. Students may break into seven groups and watch the movie for clues or traits of the Irish culture:

   - Customs,
   - Artifacts,
   - Fables and stories,
   - Rituals,
   - Beliefs,
   - Attitudes,
   - Values

Students may discuss their cultural observations after the film viewing.

Evaluation:

- Students will record their connections to the text.
- Students will memorize and recite several lines of an age-appropriate Yeats' or C.S. Lewis' poem or writing.
- Students will remember the memorized lines for life!

Challenge:

Students may:

- Write a limerick about Yeats or C.S. Lewis.

- Research about Charles Stewart Parnell and/or George Bernard Shaw to discover how their writing helped support the Irish Independence from Britain?

- Investigate James Joyce as another famous Irish writer. Students may research to find out why he is celebrated every June 16th with "Bloomsday" in Dublin. Students may cite at least two of his major works and then they may share them with your fellow classmates.

- Read about the Irish male and female monks and follow Cahill's (1995: 131) explanation on how they saved civilization. Students may describe the monk's culture and movement and their value of literature, the written word, art, and books. LLywelyn's (2010) book on Brendan will shed light on this topic as well for students.

Student Name _____   **Text Read** _____

Making Connections

Students will track and record text-to-text, text-to-world and text-to-self connections as they read W.B. Yeats or other Irish writers.

TEXT-TO-TEXT CONNECTIONS

TEXT-TO-WORLD CONNECTIONS

TEXT-TO-SELF CONNECTIONS

Lesson 19: Irish Fables and Legends

Ireland was rich in oral tradition until the monks started recording the Irish stories of the past. Like all cultural groups Irish fables and legends lend an understanding to the stories of their past.

Objective: Students will learn about at least five Irish fables, and they will be able to discuss the moral and other details for each fable.

Materials:

- o Five major Irish fables may be searched for in libraries and on the internet. Ann Carroll has adapted many fables like the five listed below. They may be ordered at: www.poolbeg.com.

Steps:

1. A teacher or group leader will order and/or collect books with the 5 Irish fables listed below.
2. Students will be divided into 5 groups.
3. The teacher will review the elements of a fable (moral, talking animals, examples of insight into a culture) with the students.
4. Each of the 5 groups will read one of the fables, answer the questions and then share their results with the whole group.
5. As individuals or in small groups, complete the Tic-Tac-Toe that follows.

The Salmon of Knowledge. Nutshell Series Adapted by Ann Carroll, Poolbeg Press Ltd. Dublin, Ireland: 2013.

Note: This fable is more suited for middle school aged students.

Middle school students will address the following questions and suggested activities:

1. Identify the 5 main characters. Discuss what happened to Fionn.
2. Explain why Fionn's father was killed.
3. Describe the warrior initiation process.
4. Surmise how Cumhall become an enemy to the Fianna.
5. Summarize Goll Mac Morna and tell how his conflict with Fionn was resolved.
6. Detail how Finnegas helped Fionn.
7. Explain the Salmon of Knowledge and discuss the elements of a fable contained in the story.
8. Retell the catching and tasting of the salmon in five detailed sentences.
9. Discuss how poetry was important to the warriors.

10. Draw a picture of Aillen and its encounter with Fionn.

11. Talk about what happened to Fionn.

The Story of the Giant's Causeway.

Students will:

1. Draw some examples of the rock formations and then explain them.

2. Describe Fionn MacCumhaill.

3. Discuss how the Giant's Causeway was created in this fable.

4. Give an account of the other giant and explain how he was deterred.

5. Identify the moral to the story.

6. List two facts and two elements of fiction from this fable.

7. Create their own fable about the Giant's Causeway and include the elements of a fable: moral message, animals, and values of a culture.

The Story of Saint Patrick.

Students will:

1. Draw and label a timeline of at least five important events in St. Patrick's life.

2. Detail how Patrick learned to speak Gaelic and describe how that language helped him.

3. Retell the three messages that God gave to Patrick?

4. Discuss how becoming a monk helped Patrick.

5. Investigate snakes in Ireland. Where they fact or fiction in this book? What could the snakes symbolize in this story?

6. Research Druids. Decide how they were a part of St. Patrick's story?

Bonus: Watch the DVD about St. Patrick (2007).

The Children of Lir.

Students will:

1. Draw a Venn diagram and compare and contrast the two queens.

2. Explain what a "kerfuffle" is.

3. Write a caption for the last illustration in the book.

4. Retell the story using only the illustrations/drawings in the book.

The Story of Newgrange

Students will:

1. Locate Newgrange on a map.

2. Identify the age of Newgrange. Locate that time on a timeline from then to the present.

3. Discuss what message from the gods they thought they saw on the inside of Newgrange?

4. Explain if winter was banished.

5. Write about what the young god did with Newgrange for a day and a night?

6. Retell how Newgrange is implicated with the winter solstice.

7. Identify the fictional characteristics in "Gods and Humans."

8. In "Changing Times," explain why Cormac didn't want to be buried with the other high kings.

9. Report what happened to Newgrange over time

10. Draw a picture of Newgrange. Discuss why a visit there might be added to your itinerary for a visit to Ireland.

Complete any three squares down, across or diagonally. Use the books referenced to complete your choice of activities.

Summarize the moral of this story in 5 detailed sentences. **The Children of Lir.**	Detail how the Winter Solstice was illustrated. **The Story of Newgrange.**	Draw examples and explain the rock formations of the Giant's Causeway. **The Story of the Giant's Causeway.**
Explain why Goll Mac Morna wanted to kill Fionn. **The Salmon of Knowledge.**	Write your own Irish fable. Include a moral to the story, and/or talking animals and an understanding of the Irish culture.	Describe at least 5 ways that God helped Patrick. **The Story of Saint Patrick.**
Give one fictional and one nonfictional explanation for the rock formations of the Giant's Causeway. **The Story of the Giant's Causeway.**	Identify supernatural elements in this story. **The Story of Saint Patrick.**	Explain what happened to Fionn in his quest to capture the "Salmon of Knowledge" from the river by the nine hazelnut trees. **The Salmon of Knowledge.**

Lesson 20: Irish Music and Dance

Have some fun with an exploration and experience of Irish Music, and then try Step Dancing.

Objective: Students will experience Irish Music and Step Dancing.

Materials:

- o Book: Wright, Robert L. (Ed.) (1975). *Irish Emigrant Ballads and Songs*. Bowling Green, Ohio: Bowling Green University Press.

DVDS:

- o Irish Dance Michael Flatley has shared with the world the wonders of Irish step dancing. See the DVD "The Best of Riverdance, 1995-2005." (Order via www.riverdance.com)

- o "Jean Butler's Irish Dance Masterclass" has step by step instructions to learn dance steps and to stay fit. Check it out at: www.kultur.com

- o Irish Step Dancing may be viewed at:
  - http://www.youtube.com/watch?v+py2TiFsa9T0
  - http://www.youtube.com/watch?v+qD6BpyHrSAA

- o Live Ireland Radio:
  - http://streema.com/radios/play/17047. Webcams show live scenes of Dublin.

Steps:

Students will:

1. Read any of the songs and ballads in *Irish Emigrant Ballads and Songs* (1975) and interpret the message. Then, students will dramatize the song's message with several friends.

2. Locate a step dancer to lead in a simple step like, "Squish the Bug."

3. Use the resources above to get on their feet and to try step dancing.

4. Experience how exhausting step dancing is! Students will check out the YouTubes listed previously and experiment with the steps!

Evaluation: All students will be on their feet and will step dance!

Lesson 21: What Have You Learned About Ireland?

Before completing the **KWLQ** chart from Lesson 1, revisit the **ABC Vocabulary** activity in Lesson 2. Refer back to the **KWLQ** chart, possibly in a folder of Irish activities. Each student will record what s/he learned about Ireland through the completion of a few or all of the activities in this book. Students will take time to share and to discuss student responses. Then, students will spend time talking about what they would like to learn in the future. The group may even devise a plan for future Irish studies!

Lesson 22: Final Challenge: Build an Ireland Itinerary

Students may have fun building a real or surreal itinerary for a visit to Ireland.

Objective: Students will plan a 14-day itinerary for a trip around Ireland. Students will allow for 16 days due to traveling one day each way with 14 days being spent in Ireland. The sixteenth day will be flying away, back home!

Materials:

- o Map of Ireland
- o Computer access
- o Example itineraries are abundant through sources like:
  - www.lonelyplanet.com/ireland
  - www.cietours.com
  - http://www.toursofireland.com/globus.cfm
  - Notes from the previous Lessons from this book about places to visit, things to do

Steps:

Students will:

1. Plan a trip together for the entire class, a small group, or a student's family.

2. Map the trip for a minimum of 14 days of touring Ireland: a total of 16 days, one day for flying each way.

3. Visit at least one of the islands: Blasket, Skellig, Aran, Raitlin, and/or Tory.

4. Stay overnight on one of the islands.

5. Experience various levels of housing: Bed & Breakfasts, Hotels, Castles and Hostels.

6. Figure out costs including transportation on the island and flying to and from Ireland.

7. Use a map of Ireland to start plotting possible routes and stops.

8. Make all of the decisions about the 16-day trip.

9. Use a computer and other resources to decide where to stay and where to go.

10. Calculate/figure all costs in Euros and Sterling if you travel to Northern Ireland.

11. Figure out what cell phone service will be purchased and add that to the costs.

12. Suggest clothing and travel gear after researching the weather.

13. Research the ethnicity and racial mix of the present Irish population.

14. Have fun!

Evaluation: Students will produce a tentative itinerary for a trip to Ireland.

It is the wish of this author that all interested parties are able to travel to Ireland at least once in their lifetime. It's true that there is something to do, whatever way a person turns in Ireland!

Please send any reviews and feedback to mesween4@gmail.com for consideration for future additions and editions. Thank you in advance!

References

Broderick, M. (1989). *History of Cobh (Queenstown) Ireland.* Cork City, Ireland: Carraig Print.

Cahill, T. (1995). *How the Irish Saved Civilization: The Untold Story of Ireland's Heroic Role from the Fall of Rome to the Rise of Medieval Europe.* New York, NY: Doubleday.

Carroll, A. (2012). *The Children of Lir.* Dublin, Ireland: Poolbeg Press Ltd.

Carroll, A. (2013a). *The Salmon of Knowledge.* Dublin, Ireland: Poolbeg Press, Ltd.

Carroll, A. (2013b). *The Story of the Giant's Causeway.* Dublin, Ireland: Poolbeg Press, Ltd.

Carroll, A. (2013c). *The Story of Newgrange.* Dublin, Ireland: Poolbeg Press, Ltd.

Carroll, A. (2013d). *The Story of Saint Patrick.* Dublin, Ireland: Poolbeg Press, Ltd.

Cartwright, R. (2011). *The Pitkin Guide to Titanic.* Andover, Hampshire: Pitkin Publishing.

Craven, R. (2009). *Spirit of the Causeway Coast.* Somerset, Great Britain.

Gaynor, Hazel (2014). *The Girl Who Came Home.* New York: Harper Collins.

Hart, A. & Mantell, P. (1998). *Knights and Castles: 50 Hands-on Activities to Explore the Middle Ages.* Nashville, TN: Williamson Publishing.

Lavelle, D. (1999). *The Skellig Story: Ancient Monastic Outpost.* Dublin, Ireland: The O'Brien Press.

Lewis, C.S. (2010 ed.). *Chronicles of Narnia: The Magician's Nephew.* New York, NY: Harper Festival.

Llywelyn, M. (1998). *1916: A Novel of the Irish Rebellion.* New York: Tom Doherty Associates.

LLywelyn, M. (2006). *The Greener Shore: A Novel of the Druids of Hibernia.* New York: Ballantine Books.

LLywelyn, M. (2010). *Brendan: The Remarkable Life and Voyage of Brendan of Clonfort.* New York: Tom Doherty Associates.

Loughrey, E. (1999). *Annie Moore: First In Line In America.* Dublin, Ireland: Mercier Press.

Maps! The World and United States. (1999). Riverside, CA: Teacher's Friend Publications, Inc.

Martin, M. (2001). *Titanic Trail.* Cork, Ireland: Collins Print and Packaging Ltd.

McKeown, A. (1996). *Titanic.* Dublin, Ireland: Poolbeg Press, Ltd.

Miller, K. & Miller, P. (2001). *Journey of Hope: The Story of Irish Immigration to America.* San Francisco, CA: Chronicle Books, LLC.

Moreton, C. (2000). *Hungry for Home: Leaving the Blaskets: A Journey from the Edge of Ireland.* New York: Penguin Putnam, Inc.

Nolan, J. (2002). *The St. Patrick's Day Shillelagh.* Morton Grove, IL: Albert Whitman & Company.

Pastore, C. (2001). Journey to America: Fiona McGilray's Story: A Voyage from Ireland in 1849. New York, New York: Berkley Jam Books.

Ready-to-Go Super Book of Outline Maps. (2000). New York, NY.: Scholastic Inc.

Scanlan, M. (2006). *Culture and Customs of Ireland.* Westport, CT: Greenwood Press.

Schneider, M. (2001). *Annie Quinn in America.* Minneapolis, MN: Carolrhoda Books, Inc.

Sibbett Jr., E. (1979). *Celtic Design Coloring Book.* Mineola, NY: Dover Publications, Inc. 1979.

Simms, G.O. (Ed.). (1986). *The Book of Kells.* England: Cheney & Sons Ltd.

Smith, R. (2016). *Michael Collins: The Big Fellow.* Dublin, Ireland: Poolbeg Press Ltd.

Spoken World Irish: A Complete Course for Beginners. (2009). New York, New York: Living Language, Random House.

Time-Life Books (Ed.), (1998). *What Life Was Like Among Druids and High Kings (Celtic Ireland AD 400-1200).* New York, New York: Time-Life Inc.

The Short Course: Speak Irish to Learn Irish. (1999). Recorded Books, LLC.

Wilson, Laura (2000). *How I Survived The Irish Famine: The Journal of Mary O'Flynn.* Dublin, Ireland: Gill & Macmillan Ltd.

Winters, E. (2006). *1-2-3 Calligraphy!* New York: Sterling Children's Books.

Wright, Robert L. (Ed.) (1975). *Irish Emigrant Ballads and Songs.* Bowling Green, Ohio: Bowling Green University Press.

Yeats, W. B. (2010 Edition). *The Celtic Twilight: Faeries and Folklore.* Las Vegas, NV: IAP.

DVDs

The Best of Riverdance, (1995-2005). Irish Dancer Michael Flatley has shared with the world the wonders of Irish step dancing. (Order via www.riverdance.com)

*Jimmy's Hall. (*2014) PG-13. For Middle School students

Patrick, (2007). Liam Neeson narrator, For Middle School students

Secret of Roan Innish. (1994). PG, For elementary age students with a caution of a nude baby

The Wind That Shakes the Barley. (2005). PG-13, For Middle School Students

9780990775928